Margery; or, a worse plague than the dragon: a burlesque opera. As it is perform'd at the Theatre-Royal in Covent-Garden. Altered from the original Italian of Signor Carini. Set to musick by Mr. John-Frederick Lampe.

Henry Carey

PRINT EDITIONS

Eighteenth Century
Collections Online
Print Editions

Gale ECCO Print Editions

Relive history with *Eighteenth Century Collections Online*, now available in print for the independent historian and collector. This series includes the most significant English-language and foreign-language works printed in Great Britain during the eighteenth century, and is organized in seven different subject areas including literature and language; medicine, science, and technology; and religion and philosophy. The collection also includes thousands of important works from the Americas.

The eighteenth century has been called "The Age of Enlightenment." It was a period of rapid advance in print culture and publishing, in world exploration, and in the rapid growth of science and technology – all of which had a profound impact on the political and cultural landscape. At the end of the century the American Revolution, French Revolution and Industrial Revolution, perhaps three of the most significant events in modern history, set in motion developments that eventually dominated world political, economic, and social life.

In a groundbreaking effort, Gale initiated a revolution of its own: digitization of epic proportions to preserve these invaluable works in the largest online archive of its kind. Contributions from major world libraries constitute over 175,000 original printed works. Scanned images of the actual pages, rather than transcriptions, recreate the works *as they first appeared.*

Now for the first time, these high-quality digital scans of original works are available via print-on-demand, making them readily accessible to libraries, students, independent scholars, and readers of all ages.

For our initial release we have created seven robust collections to form one the world's most comprehensive catalogs of 18th century works.

Initial Gale ECCO Print Editions collections include:

History and Geography
Rich in titles on English life and social history, this collection spans the world as it was known to eighteenth-century historians and explorers. Titles include a wealth of travel accounts and diaries, histories of nations from throughout the world, and maps and charts of a world that was still being discovered. Students of the War of American Independence will find fascinating accounts from the British side of conflict.

Social Science

Delve into what it was like to live during the eighteenth century by reading the first-hand accounts of everyday people, including city dwellers and farmers, businessmen and bankers, artisans and merchants, artists and their patrons, politicians and their constituents. Original texts make the American, French, and Industrial revolutions vividly contemporary.

Medicine, Science and Technology

Medical theory and practice of the 1700s developed rapidly, as is evidenced by the extensive collection, which includes descriptions of diseases, their conditions, and treatments. Books on science and technology, agriculture, military technology, natural philosophy, even cookbooks, are all contained here.

Literature and Language

Western literary study flows out of eighteenth-century works by Alexander Pope, Daniel Defoe, Henry Fielding, Frances Burney, Denis Diderot, Johann Gottfried Herder, Johann Wolfgang von Goethe, and others. Experience the birth of the modern novel, or compare the development of language using dictionaries and grammar discourses.

Religion and Philosophy

The Age of Enlightenment profoundly enriched religious and philosophical understanding and continues to influence present-day thinking. Works collected here include masterpieces by David Hume, Immanuel Kant, and Jean-Jacques Rousseau, as well as religious sermons and moral debates on the issues of the day, such as the slave trade. The Age of Reason saw conflict between Protestantism and Catholicism transformed into one between faith and logic -- a debate that continues in the twenty-first century.

Law and Reference

This collection reveals the history of English common law and Empire law in a vastly changing world of British expansion. Dominating the legal field is the *Commentaries of the Law of England* by Sir William Blackstone, which first appeared in 1765. Reference works such as almanacs and catalogues continue to educate us by revealing the day-to-day workings of society.

Fine Arts

The eighteenth-century fascination with Greek and Roman antiquity followed the systematic excavation of the ruins at Pompeii and Herculaneum in southern Italy; and after 1750 a neoclassical style dominated all artistic fields. The titles here trace developments in mostly English-language works on painting, sculpture, architecture, music, theater, and other disciplines. Instructional works on musical instruments, catalogs of art objects, comic operas, and more are also included.

The BiblioLife Network

This project was made possible in part by the BiblioLife Network (BLN), a project aimed at addressing some of the huge challenges facing book preservationists around the world. The BLN includes libraries, library networks, archives, subject matter experts, online communities and library service providers. We believe every book ever published should be available as a high-quality print reproduction; printed on-demand anywhere in the world. This insures the ongoing accessibility of the content and helps generate sustainable revenue for the libraries and organizations that work to preserve these important materials.

The following book is in the "public domain" and represents an authentic reproduction of the text as printed by the original publisher. While we have attempted to accurately maintain the integrity of the original work, there are sometimes problems with the original work or the micro-film from which the books were digitized. This can result in minor errors in reproduction. Possible imperfections include missing and blurred pages, poor pictures, markings and other reproduction issues beyond our control. Because this work is culturally important, we have made it available as part of our commitment to protecting, preserving, and promoting the world's literature.

GUIDE TO FOLD-OUTS MAPS and OVERSIZED IMAGES

The book you are reading was digitized from microfilm captured over the past thirty to forty years. Years after the creation of the original microfilm, the book was converted to digital files and made available in an online database.

In an online database, page images do not need to conform to the size restrictions found in a printed book. When converting these images back into a printed bound book, the page sizes are standardized in ways that maintain the detail of the original. For large images, such as fold-out maps, the original page image is split into two or more pages

Guidelines used to determine how to split the page image follows:

• Some images are split vertically; large images require vertical and horizontal splits.
• For horizontal splits, the content is split left to right.
• For vertical splits, the content is split from top to bottom.
• For both vertical and horizontal splits, the image is processed from top left to bottom right.

MARGERY;

OR, A

Worfe Plague than the DRAGON:

A Burlefque OPERA.

As it is Perform'd at the

THEATRE-ROYAL in *Covent-Garden.*

Altered from the Original Italian *of*
Signor CARINI.

Set to MUSICK

By Mr JOHN-FREDERICK LAMPE.

LONDON.

Printed for J. SHUCKBURGH, at the *Sun* near the
Inner-Temple-Gate in *Fleet-ftreet*, 1738.
(Price Six-pence.)

MARGERY

OR, A

Worse Plague than the DRAGON:

A Burlesque O P E R A.

[Price 6*d*.]

DRAMATIS PERSONÆ.

Moore *of* Moore-Hall,	Mr. SALWAY.
Gaffar Gubbins, *Father to Lady* Moore,	Mr. LAGUERRE.
Lady Moore, *formerly* Margery Gubbins,	Mrs. LAMPE.
Mauxalinda,	Miss ESTHER YOUNG.
Herald,	Mr. REINHOLD.
First Guest,	Mr. ROBERTS.

CHORUS *of Priests, Huntsmen, Guests, &c. Constable, Jailor, Pursuivants, Guards, and other Attendants.*

SCENE, Yorkshire.

The ARGUMENT.

MAUXALINDA, *enraged at the Falshood of* MOORE, *retires disconsolate to a Desart, unable to bear the Triumphs of her Rival* MARGERY *(now Lady* MOORE) *who from the meekest of Creatures, is so elevated with her present Grandeur, that she becomes a very* Virago, *a worse Plague than the Dragon; and leads her Husband such a confounded Life, that he runs away from her on the very Wedding-Night, and flies, for Quiet-sake, to the Desart; where meeting with* MAUXALINDA, *they renew their former Loves, and grow fonder than ever. Lady* MOORE *pursues them with the utmost Fury, surprizes them in the height of their Endearments, and sends* MAUXALINDA *to* Prison. MOORE *makes a second Elopement, and sends* GUBBINS *to release* MAUXALINDA; *which being done,* GUBBINS, *who has long loved her in secret, courts her, and gains her Consent.* MOORE

wants

The ARGUMENT.

to renew his former Acquaintance with MAUXALINDA, *but is repuls'd by her, and furiously attack'd by his Lady: After a smart Scolding-Bout they make it up:* MOORE *is friends with his Lady;* GUBBINS *is married to* MAUXALINDA; *and the Opera concludes, according to the Custom of all Operas, with the general Reconciliation of all Parties, no matter how absurd, improbable, or ridiculous.*

DRA.

MARGERY;
OR, A
Worse Plague than the DRAGON.

ACT I. SCENE I.

*A Magnificent Temple finely illumi-
nated, a great Number of Priests,
Choristers, &c. Bride-Men, Bride-
Maids, &c. &c. Moore and his
Lady, Gubbins, Guests, Guards, and
other Attendants, &c. &c. &c.*

CHORUS.

*Triumph Valour, triumph Beauty,
Fortune now has done its Duty.*

RECITATIVE.

Moore. OW to *Moore-Hall*, my
Friends, let's haste away,
To celebrate this happy
Nuptial-Day.

Cho. *Triumph, Valour, &c*   [Exeunt,

B   SCENE

SCENE II. *A Defart.*

MAUXALINDA *fola.*

From *Moore*, and my too happy Rival flown,
Poor *Mauxalinda* wanders here alone.
Their Bridal Joys are worfe than Death to me.
Alas! how cruel is my Deftiny !

A I R.

The Swain I adore has undone me,
He woo'd me until he had won me :
He courted me, fure, but to fhun me,
And now from his Arms am I thrown.

Come Death, from Diftraction relieve me,
Cold Earth to thy Bofom receive me ;
Come thou who fo bafely could'ft leave me,
And fhed one kind Tear on my Stone.

[Exit.

SCENE III. Moore-Hall.

MOORE *and his Lady,* GUBBINS, *Guefts,&c.*
An Entertainment of Dancing; after
which, enter Herald, Purfuivants, &c.

Herald Moft puiffant *Moore !* Our Sovereign
Lord the King
Hearing your Fame, which far and near doth
ring,
Sends you this Token of his Royal Bounty,
[*Puts on a Golden Helmet.*
And

And makes you Lord-Lieutenant of the County :

A *Dragon paſſant guardant* is your Arms.

And hearing of your Conſort's peerleſs Charms,

Invites to Court both you and Lady *Moore*,

Where he has farther Honours yet in ſtore.

Moore. My kind Love to his Majeſty, I pray :

We'll juſt keep Honey-moon, and then away.

[Exit *Herald*, &c.

Moore. How comes it *Mauxalinda* is not here,

[*Surveying the Company.*

To grace our Nuptials, and partake our Cheer ?

Lady. Methinks, in Manners, you might longer ſtay ;

Can't you forget her on your Wedding-Day ?

Ungrateful, ——

Gub. —— Daughter, ſet your Fears aſide,

For *Mauxalinda*, mad with Rage and Pride ;

Has, in a Hurry, pack'd up all her Things,

Her Cloaths, her Money, nay, her three Gold Rings,

And went away this Morning by the Carrier.

Moore. She's a ſmart Girl, ſome *Londoner* may marry her.

AIR.

A I R.

Thus the Damsel young and pretty,
Quits the Country with Disdain,
Takes a Trip to London *City,*
Nobler Conquests to obtain.

There she Prudes it so demurely,
And so well displays her Charms,
That some Townling, most securely,
She allures into her Arms.

Lady. All this is meer Contrivance and Deceit
  With half an Eye I can see through the
  Cheat.

A I R.

Go, Cuckoldly Cull,
  Follow your Trull.
I'm not to be made such a Tool.
Sir Knight, I'm your Wife,
  And, during my Life,
Your Worship shall find me no Fool.

Moore. I'm all Surprize! What means this sud-
  den Change!
  'Tis wond'rous odd!
Gub —'Tis more than odd, 'tis strange!
Moore Speak to her, Sir —
Gub. ——— Not I, upon my Life:
  'Tis dangerous medling betwixt Man and
  Wife.

A I R

A I R.

Agree, agree ;
If not, d'ye see,
As you fall out,
Fall in, for me.

Moore Why is my deareſt Dear ſo croſs to me?
I wou'd not be ſo to my *Margery*.
Lady. It might be *Marg'ry Gubbins* heretofore ;
But now I'll make you know I'm Lady
Moore.   [*Strutting.*
Moore. Why ſo thou art : — But yet I hope,
my Dear,   [*Coaxing.*
If thou art Cap, I may be Button here.
Lady. You think you're Maſter now; but that
won't do,
I tell you, I'll be Cap and Button too.
Moore. My Anger riſes . — Woman, have a care !
Lady. I ſcorn your Anger. — Strike me if you
dare !

A I R.

You! You! You!
Coxcomb! Blockhead! Numpskull' Nizey!
I defy you ' I deſpiſe you!
Do! Do! Do ! —   [*Exit Lady.*
Moore. Are theſe the Joys of Wedlock! This
the Life
A Man muſt lead with an outrageous Wife ?
Gub. Son ! keep your Temper ; — Let her have
her Way,
Brides know their Power on their Wedding-
Day.   The

The Joys they give us wou'd be too com-
  pleat,
Did not some Bitter mingle with the Sweet.
This is some female Flight, some jealous Fit.
Moore. You see, my Friends, how 'tis; — I
  must submit.

A I R.

So Hercules *of old,*
   The Valiant and the Bold,   (rue,
Who made the fierce Giants and Monsters to
   Was forc'd to rock and reel,
   And turn the Spinning-Wheel;
So much cou'd a Woman his Passion subdue.
            So Hercules, &c.   [Exit.

Gub. Farewell, *Moore-Hall,* thou art no Place
  for Stay :
  O, Friends' this is a dismal Wedding-Day !

Melancholy C H O R U S.

   Oh sad ! oh strange !
   Oh doleful Change !
         Oh, &c.   [Exeunt Omnes.

                                   A C T

ACT II. SCENE I.
A Defart.

MOORE *folus.*

FArewell, *Moore-Hall*— I now have broke
    my Chain,
I never more will darken thee again. (Devil;
This Woman has a Spirit wou'd fcare the
Tygers and Wolves, compar'd to her, are civil.
Alas! what mighty Deeds have I to brag on?
I'm móre afraid of her, than of the Dragon.
Sooner in Defarts with wild Beafts I'll dwell,
Than with that Wife, who makes my Home
    a Hell.

A I R.

Was ever Man fo much deceiv'd?
Can ever Woman be believ'd?
   I thought my Love
    a Turtle-Dove,
And dream'd of endlefs Charms,
   But now I've got,
   O curfed Lot!
A Dragon to my Arms.
         Was ever, &c
           Maux.

Maux. Cruel Swain !—— [*Behind the Scenes.*
Moore. What tender, plaintive Sounds invade
    my Ear?
Sure Melancholy's self inhabits here:
Approach, sweet Warbler! thou perhaps
    may'st be   (me ;
Some easy cred'lous Wretch, deceiv'd like
I'll not obstruct, but listen to thy Moan,
Then mingle, with thy soft Complaints, my
   own.
      [*Retires to a Corner of the Stage.*

    Enter MAUXALINDA.

      A I R.

Cruel Swain, since you forsake me,
I'll to lonely Shades betake me,
   Like the mournful Turtle-Dove ·

While my Fondness you're disdaining,
Faithful still in soft complaining,
   I'll lament my hapless Love.
        Cruel Swain, &c

     [Moore *coming forward, and dif-*
     covering himself
My *Mauxalinda!* O transporting Sight
Come to my Arms, thou Treasure of Delight
     [*Goes to embrace her, she flies back*
          Maux.

Maux. What new Device is this, to mock my
    Grief?

Experience now has banifh'd all Belief.

Moore. I own my Crime , O pardon my Of-
    fence ;

I'm all Confufion, Shame and Penitence.

                         [*Kneeling.*

Maux. O *Moore!* I lov'd you as I did my
    Life——

I'd fain believe you, but you've got a Wife

Moore Oh! name her not — With thee, my
    Love, I'll fly

Far as the utmoft Verge of Earth or Sky :

We'll traverfe ev'ry Sea, and ev'ry Shore,

And ne'er approach that hated Object more.

            D U E T T O.

Around the wide World we will wander,

Grow fonder, and fonder, and fonder ,

    We'll cuddle together,

    To keep out the Weather,

And kifs the cold Winter away.

When Sol's *fultry Heat does invade us,*

Green Ofiers and Willows fhall fhade us.

    We'll chirrip and fing

    Like Birds in the Spring,

And frolick it all the long Day.

           Around, &c. [Exeunt.

C   S C E N E

SCENE II. Gubbins's *House*.

Gubbins *and Guests as from Drinking.*

1st Guest. Thanks, noble *Gubbins*, for this
 Night's Repast :——
I think we've fairly made it out at last.
Gub But why so hasty, why so soon away?
 Another Bottle will bring on the Day.

Enter Lady MOORE.

Gub. What's this I see?— My Daughter !—
 Say, my Dear!
What brings thee thus unseasonably here?
How could'st thou quit so soon the Bridal
 Bed?   *[Lady sighs*
A Sigh too! Tell me, is thy Husband dead?
Lady. Oh! ten times worse!
Gub. ——— How can that be?
Lady. ——— He's fled.
Gub. What! before Consummation?
Lady. Ay, to my great Vexation.
Gub. O Daughter, Daughter! if I right con-
 jecture,
He ran away, to 'scape a Curtain-Lecture.
        Lady

Lady. No, he has *Mauxalinda* in his Mind :
Now she is gone, he cannot stay behind.

A I R.

Wretched is a Wife's Condition,
When not Rage, or yet Submission,
Can reclaim her faithless Rover,
Or to Virtue bring him over.

When she sees her self neglected,
And her Rival more respected,
Oh! how great must be her Anguish!
Who can blame her then to languish.
       Wretched, &c

Gub. He's sadly off; for she, like thee, I fear,
May have a Tongue too many for his Ear.
Lady. Unhappy me! I came to be redrest,
And you, I see, make all my Wrongs your
  Jest:
But I'll, through all the Courts of Law pur-
  sue him;
I'll rumage Hell it self, but I'll undo him:
I'll issue out Reward by Proclamation,
And have him, if he's living in the Nation.
        [*Exit*
Gub. Well said, my Girl— thy Mother's
  Daughter still;
She had a Tongue most exquisitely shrill.
        [*Horn sounds.*
    C 2   But

But hárk! the jolly Huntfman's Hötn
Gives Notice of approaching Morn:
Let's lofe no Moment of Delight,
But hunt all Day, as we have drank all
   Night.

A I R.

Come follow, braʋe Boys, to the Chace,
   For Morning breaks on us apace;
The Fogs and the Miſt diſappear,
   The Dawn is delightfully clear.
The Hounds are uncoupled, then haſt and
   away,
You'll loſe all the Sport, if you longer de-
   lay.
What, what are your Opera's to me,
But Tweedlecum-Tweedlecum-twee:
No Muſick, that's under the Sky,
Can equal the Hounds at full Cry.
Then a Fig for Italians, *their Squeak and*
   their Squawl,
One true Engliſh *Sportſman ſhall dumb-*
   found'em all.

Omnes, Hiddow, &c.

[*Exeunt*

S C E N E

SCENE III. *The Defart.*

MOORE *and* MAUXALINDA *embracing.*

DUETTO.

Maux. *By thefe Arms, that round thee twine.*
  Like the ever-circling Vine :
  By this tender fond Embrace,
  Nothing ſhall my Love efface.

Moore. *By the Nectar, which I ſip*
  From thy ſoft and ruby Lip,
  Never, never will I leave thee,
  Never, never more deceive thee.

Enter Lady MOORE *with Conſtable, Guards,*
  &c. *and ſurprizes 'em.*

Lady. So, ſo, my pretty Turtles, are you
  there——

  I've caught you napping, as *Moſs* caught
  his Mare.

  Sir, that's your Priſoner—— [*To Conſtable.*
  Now, my Lady Stock,   [*To* Maux.
  You ſhall *mill Dolley* at the Hempen-Block.

   [Mauxalinda *is carried off*; Moore
   ſtrives to follow, but is pre-
   vented by his Lady.

          For

For you, Sir Knight, come Home, and
   mind your Duty;
I'll teach you to run rambling after Beauty.

DUETTO.

Lady. *O ungrateful ! to deceive me,*
   Thus to rob me of Content.
Moore. *O moſt hateful ! leave me, leave me;*
   You my Anger but augment.
Lady. *Faithleſs Traytor !*
Moore. *Plague of Nature !*
Lady. *Where's your Conſcience ?*
Moore. *Curſe your Nonſenſe !*
   Let me go, Let me go. [Struggling.
Lady. *No, no, no ; No, no, no.*
       O ungrateful, &c.

         [Exeunt.

ACT

ACT III. SCENE I.

GUBBINS'S *House.*

GUBBINS *and* MOORE.

Moore. OH, Sir! here's been a moſt con-
          founded Rout——

  Mauxy's in Hold, and you muſt bring her out.

  As ſhe and I, like Turtles of a feather,

  Were cooing in the Wilderneſs together,

  My Lady came with *Poſſé Comitatus,*

  And ſent poor *Mauxalinda* to the Gate-
    houſe.

Gub Why, 'tis a thing no Wife alive can bear,

  To have another in her Husband ſhare.

Moore. Sir, with her ſpotleſs Virtue you're
    too free,

  For *Mauxalinda's* ſtill a Maid, for me.

  Our Meeting was mere Accident and Chance;

  What you think Courtſhip, was but Com-
    plaiſance.

  O joyful Tidings! I am ſtill ſecure,

                    [Gubbins *aſide.*

  And *Mauxalinda* is a Virgin pure.

                        [To *Moore.*

I

I cannot bear she should a Prisoner be——
I'll tear the Jail down, but I'll set her free.

[*Exit.*

MOORE *solus.*

Was ever Man so hamper'd with a Wife?
Patience, ye Gods! but I am link'd for Life:
The Knot's too fast, 'tis needless to complain;
I wish the *Dragon* were alive again.

A I R.

The Lion in Battle engag'd,
When he fills all the Forest with Dread,
Is a Lamb to a Woman enrag'd,
If once Jealousy gets in her Head.

Her Soul's on a Ferment of Fury,
No soothing the Tempest can still;
She values no Law, Judge or Jury,
Her darling Revenge to fulfill.

[Exit.

SCENE II. *A Prison.*

MAUXALINDA *in Chains.*

A I R.
O piercing Anguish!
O cruel Destiny!
Here must I languish
For Loss of Liberty.

[Enter Lady *Moore.*
So,

So, Madam, — How d'ye like your stately
 Lodging?
Is not this better than in Defarts dodging?
I hope you're fixt fo well, you ne'er will roam ;
We're fure to find you always now at Home.

Maux. Madam, I fee through all your faucy
 Sneer ——
You may provoke my Scorn, but not my
 Fear.

Lady. Your boafted Courage I'm refolv'd to try,
Behold this Dagger, and prepare to die.

      [*Draws a Dagger.*

D U E T T O.

Maux. *Since you've robb'd me of my Trea-*
 fure,
Life is now no more a Pleafure :
Death is welcome ev'n from you.

Lady. *Since you've robb'd me of my Treafure,*
In your Death is all my Pleafure .
Vengeance, Vengeance is my Due.

[*Enter* Gubbins *with Jailor and Guards.*

Daughter, forbear, and let your Fury ceafe ;
For know I'm come poor *Mauxy* to releafe.
To Jailor.] Here's her Difcharge, Sir, from a
 Juftice o' Peace.

    D   *Lady.*

Lady. My Father too my Foe! Patience is vain.

Gub. *Marg'ry* thy Pride, I think, has turn'd
    thy Brain.

Lady I'll be reveng'd ——

Gub. ————Nay, if she makes a Riot,
                           [*To Jailor.*
  Jailor, secure her, 'till she grows more quiet
                 [*Ex.* Gub. Maux. &c.

       Lady MOORE *sola.*

This is enough to make a Woman mad ——
I'll be reveng'd, if Vengeance can be had.

          A I R.

   Thus distracted, thus tormented,
     Nothing shall my Rage delay;
   Never will I rest contented
    'Till my Vengeance makes it way.
                  [Exit *Lady.*

SCENE III. Gubbins's *House.*

   MAUXALINDA *and* GUBBINS.

Maux. This wond'rous Goodness how can I
    repay!

Gub. Oh! you shall make it up another way.
       [*Chucking her under the Chin.*
Sweet *Mauxalinda,* if you can forsake
All other Men for Gaffar *Gubbins'* sake,
And prove to him a true and faithful Wife,
With all I have I'll Jointure thee for Life.
                A I R.

AIR.

Mauxalinda *thus admiring,*
 Does my Soul of Souls inslave;
For her Charm of Charms expiring,
 See her fond Adorer crave.

      [*Lady* Moore *over-hearing.*

Lady. This am'rous Scene is fure paft all Belief,

And moves my Laughter in the midft of
 Grief.

Maux. Since they've depriv'd me of my deareft Knight,   [*Afide.*

I'll marry *Gubbins* merely out of Spight.

And when I'm Madam *Marg'ry's* Mother-in-
 Law,

By *Jove*, I'll keep her Ladyfhip in awe.

     [*Turns to* Gubbins, *and fings.*

AIR.

Then come to my Arms, old Dad,
And fondle thine own dear Honey:
If Love is too late to be had,
Let's make up the Lofs with Money.

      [They Embrace.

   [*To them Lady* MOORE.

Lady. Why Father, what d'ye mean ?

Gub.———— What's that to you?

I'm old enough to know what 'tis I do.

   D 3   *Lady.*

Lady. To have more Wit, you're old enough,
    'tis true,

And she has Wit enough to Cuckold you.

Gub Audacious Hussy ! don't my Rage provoke.

Lady. I'm sure she only takes you for a Cloak.

Maux How, Madam Pert ! I'll make you know
    hereafter,

That I'm your Father's Wife, and you're my
    Daughter.

Lady. Vain Wretch! — You Mother to my
    Lady *Moore!*

Gub. Daughter, this Usage is not to be bore.

Lady Why sure you can't so great a Bubble be !--

But none so blind as those who will not see.

By *Moore* deserted, desp'rate was her Case;

She thought you fittest to supply his Place.

        Enter MOORE.

O joyful Sight! my *Mauxalinda* freed !

Thanks noble *Gubbins* for this gen'rous Deed.

O let me clasp thee to my Arms.

            [*Runs to embrace her.*
            [Gubbins *interposing.*

Gub. ———————Not so———

She's now My *Mauxalinda,* you must know

Moore What can this mean ? Is't possible !

Maux —————— — ———— — 'Tis true.

Harrass'd and plagu'd betwixt your Wife and
    you,

                   Rather

Rather than I'd incur the Old Maid's Curse,
I've taken Him for better and for worse.

      [*Lady comes up to* Moore.

Lady. How can you bear the Loss of one so dear?

Moore. My Plague! my Bane! my Evil Genius here!

Lady. Why don't it put its Finger in its Eye,
 And, like a Baby, for its Play-thing cry?

Moore. Fly, thou detested Object, fly my Sight!

Lady. I come, Sir, to demand you as my Right.

Moore. Of me you shall have nothing but the
 Name.

Lady. Has then a Wife no Marriage-Rites to
 claim?

 No Nuptial Kindness? ———

Moore.———————Not one single Kiss.

Lady. Barbarian, did'st thou marry me for this?

Moore. With Hopes of Bliss, I took thee to my
 Arms;

 But your curst Tongue has blasted all your
 Charms;

 Henceforth no Husband hope to find of me,
 'Till you more gentle and submissive be.
 Beneath one Roof, with each a sep'rate Bed,
 We'll live polite — and wish each other dead.

       [*Lady aside.*

        Lady.

Lady. A lonely Life in fep'rate Beds to 'lead,——
  Cruel Decree; better be dead indeed.
  But this I have deferv'd; and find too late,
  Iv'e brought upon my felf this Stroke of Fate.

  [To Moore.

  O, Sir! your Looks, your Words have riv'd my
      Heart —— —
  No other Way to punifh, but to part? —
  See at your Feet, your Pardon I implore;
  I never will provoke your Anger more.

Moore. What Farce is this! ———

Lady.———————No Farce, my deareft Life,
  But a Converted and Obedient Wife.

A I R.

Never, never I'll offend you,
  Or your warm Refentment dare.
Ever, ever I'll attend you,
  Your Content fhall crown my Care.

Moore. Come to my Arms, thou Treafure of
      my Life,
  Henceforth my beft belov'd, and deareft Wife.

Lady. Duty has left me yet another Task,
  Which is a double Pardon here to ask.

  [Turning to Gubbins and Mauxalinda.

Gub. You have it Child: *Maux,* As witnefs
  this Embrace.   [*They embrace.*

Moore. Methinks I fee a Smile in ev'ry Face.

D U E T T O.

DUETTO.

O happy Transformation !
O sweet Reconciliation !
O joyous blest Event !

Moore. And now, my *Marg'ry*, may'st thou
ever be   [*Embracing Lady* Moore.
As kind to *Moore*, as he is fond of thee.

Maux. I wish you Joy, Sir ! May she ever be
As true to you— as you have been to me.
                              [*Aside.*

Gub. Why now all's right.—— Call all the
Country in ;
Keep Open-House, and let the Sports begin.
[*An Entertainment of Dancing ; after-*
wards Moore *comes forward.*

Moore. Henceforth let Discord and Dissention
cease,
While we all live in Harmony and Peace.

Gub. And have of Wealth and Children great
Increase.

CHORUS.

Strain your Voices, crack your Strings.
He sings best, who loudest sings
Blow your Cheeks of Sound away,
This most Glorious Holiday.

CHORUS

CHORUS OF CHORUSSES.

BRAVO!

BRAVISSIMO!

CARO!

CARISSIMO!

A———H!

DOLCE!

BELLA!

VIVA!

ENCORE!

Da Capo.

Il FINE.

CPSIA information can be obtained at www.ICGtesting.com
Printed in the USA
267447BV00002B/120/P

9 781170 050514